ZOMBIES

BY SUE HAMILTON

Visit us at
WWW.ABDOPUBLISHING.COM

Published by ABDO Publishing Company, 4940 Viking Drive, Suite 622, Edina, Minnesota 55435.
Copyright ©2007 by Abdo Consulting Group, Inc. International copyrights reserved in all countries.
No part of this book may be reproduced in any form without written permission from the publisher.
ABDO & Daughters™ is a trademark and logo of ABDO Publishing Company.

Printed in the United States.

Editors: John Hamilton/Tad Bornhoft
Graphic Design: Sue Hamilton
Cover Design: Neil Klinepier
Cover Illustration: Zombies art, Corbis
Interior Photos and Illustrations: p 1 Detail zombies art, Corbis; p 5 Zombies art, Corbis; p 6 Map of Hispaniola, Hargrett; p 7 Voodoo artifacts, Corbis; p 8 Haitian snake charmer, Corbis; p 9 Human skull with top hat, Corbis; pp 10-11 Human skulls at a voodoo temple, Corbis; p 12 Tomb of Marie Laveau, AP/Wideworld; p 13 Voodoo queen, Corbis; p 14 Puffer fish, courtesy Marine Biological Laboratory; p 15 (top) Marine toad, Corbis; (bottom) Hyla tree frog, Corbis; p 17 Felicia Felix-Mentor, Mary Evans; p 18 Modern voodoo priest, Corbis; p 19 Cemetery in Haiti, Corbis; p 20 Man with yaws, courtesy Tropical Medicine Central Resource; pp 20-21 Overcrowded street in Africa, Corbis; p 21 Advanced yaws on legs, courtesy Tropical Medicine Central Resource; p 22 *White Zombie,* courtesy United Artists; p 23 George A. Romero, AP/Wideworld; *Night of the Living Dead,* courtesy Image Ten; *Dawn of the Dead,* courtesy Laurel Group; *Day of the Dead,* courtesy Dead Films Inc.; *Land of the Dead,* courtesy Universal Pictures; p 24 (top and bottom) Actors having zombie make-up applied, Corbis; p 25 *Shaun of the Dead* poster, courtesy Universal Pictures; p 26 *Resident Evil* package and screen shot, courtesy Capcom; p 27 *Stubbs the Zombie* screen shots, courtesy Aspyr Media and Wideload Games; *Zombies!!!®,* courtesy Twilight Creations, Inc.; p 28 *The Magic Island,* courtesy Paragon House; *The Zombie Survival Guide,* courtesy Gerald Duckworth & Co Ltd; p 29 *Marvel Zombies* book cover and images used with permission from Marvel Entertainment, Inc.; p 31 Michael Jackson and dancers, Corbis; *Shaun of the Dead* poster, courtesy Universal Pictures

Library of Congress Cataloging-in-Publication Data

Hamilton, Sue L., 1959-
  Zombies / Sue Hamilton.
      p. cm. -- (The world of horror)
  Includes index.
  ISBN-13: 978-1-59928-777-5
  ISBN-10: 1-59928-777-3
  1. Zombies. I. Title.

GR581.H36 2007
398'.45--dc22

                    2006032746

AR PTS: 1.0

CONTENTS

WHAT IS A ZOMBIE?

A zombie is a person who is neither dead nor alive—the undead. In folklore, zombies are walking corpses. They have died, but have been awakened through supernatural means. The rotting cadavers seek out the living, intent on killing and eating the humans they find. In some stories, zombies especially want to eat human brains.

As part of the voodoo (also called vodou) religion, zombies are people who are either dead or alive, but now walk the earth with no soul or will of their own. A bokor, or black magician, is their master. These zombies do whatever is commanded of them, doomed to an existence of servitude as uncomplaining workers, and sometimes as killers.

The term zombie seems to originate from the African word "nzambi," or "god." The Grand Serpent ("Le Grand Zombi") was the father of all "loas," or gods. He appeared in the shape of a large python. Dangerous and unpredictable, this loa could only be controlled by a strong magician. If the summoner was not powerful enough, the loa could take revenge upon the black magician. However, in another form of voodoo, the meaning is different. A zombie is someone who has been taken over by a loa, whether the person is dead or alive. From this concept it is likely that the Western idea of walking corpses arose.

Can a person be turned into a zombie? Some say that all it takes is the power of suggestion. If you believe, it can happen. Others say it requires the skilled knowledge of a black magician, someone who knows how powerful poisons work in and on the human body. Whether reality or fiction, zombies will always be popular characters in the world of horror.

Above: Artistic illustration of zombies shuffling up a hill near Hollywood, California.

HAITI VOODOO

The religion of voodoo and the concept of zombies began in Africa and traveled with captured slaves to the Caribbean island of Haiti, which was a busy slave center in the 1700s. Many thousands of slaves worked on French plantations in Haiti. Fearing the native Africans' voodoo practices, the French taught the slaves the Roman Catholic religion.

As the slaves learned Catholicism, their two religions merged in several ways. To the slaves, many of the loas (gods) seemed much like the Christian saints. For example, Legba is the loa who controls gates, fences and entryways, while the Christian Saint Peter is the gatekeeper of heaven. Vodounists did not think that combining religions was bad, but rather added to their faith. That belief was not shared by the white priests and landowners. Anyone caught practicing voodoo was imprisoned, whipped, or hanged. At one point, slaves were even forbidden to gather together in groups.

Instead of ending voodoo, these punishments led many slaves to continue practicing their religion in secret. In turn, those who practiced voodoo often turned from the gods of love and goodwill to "black magic," where evil spirits were called on for evil purposes. Houngans (voodoo priests) and bokors (paid priests) used their black magic to cause bad luck, illness, death, and even to turn people into zombies. Knowledge of these black arts spread rapidly.

Slaves, especially those whose owners were afraid of them, were often sold to people in North America. New Orleans, Louisiana, and Charleston, South Carolina, became voodoo centers. People of all skin colors visited the often-frightening world of the vodounists in search of everything from curses to cures to love potions.

Facing Page: Voodoo artifacts. *Below:* A 17th-century map of the island of Hispaniola. Haiti is on the western part of the island. Today, the Dominican Republic occupies the other side.

VOODOO KING

In the 1800s, New Orleans, Louisiana, was a hotbed of voodoo activity. Some feared the strange, supernatural religion, while others were drawn to it. The voodoo queens and priestesses and the male hóungans or babalawo—fathers of secrets—became both famous and infamous.

Dr. John Montenet

Dr. John Montenet, also known as Dr. John Croix, Voodoo John, and Bayou John, was reportedly a prince from Senegal, Africa, who had been captured by slavers. Eventually, he earned his freedom and became a voodoo priest.

As a tall, heavily tattooed man of color, Dr. John projected a convincing, as well as frightening, sense of power. Montenet conducted business privately in his New Orleans home. This house of horror was filled with all manner of voodoo materials—human and animal skulls, bones, snakes, toads, embalmed scorpions, herbs, and charms. Many people were convinced that Dr. John's powers were real, and were willing to pay him to tell their future, cast spells, and cure illnesses. He became quite wealthy.

However, his powers also extended to black magic. It was known that he owned his own slaves. Several were supposedly zombies.

Facing Page: A human skull with a top hat. The display was in a voodoo museum in New Orleans.
Right: A Haitian snake charmer in Port-au-Prince, Haiti.

These "living dead" were rumored to work around Montenet's home, as well as handle the evil and grisly errands of their voodoo master. Some say it was the zombie slaves who were sent by Voodoo John to local cemeteries to dig up and steal corpses. Where else could Dr. John get his constant supply of human skulls?

In private, however, John reportedly laughed with friends at the amount of money he charged for his fake voodoo magic. Perhaps this caused his own curse.

Below: Human skulls adorn a voodoo temple in Haiti.

As Montenet aged, he decided to learn to read and write, and employed a young man to help him. Dr. John was instructed to practice writing his name on sheets of paper. Without knowing it, the voodoo priest signed away most of his money, as well as his home.

Although he tried to regain his voodoo status, he discovered that younger people had taken over his business. One young woman had even trained with him, and her reputation became even greater than Dr. John's.

VOODOO QUEEN

Mystery flowed through the dark rooms and back streets of 18th and 19th century New Orleans, Louisiana. Into this era came the city's future voodoo queen. Marie Laveau was probably born in 1794 in New Orleans, Louisiana. Marie's mother was a mulatto woman, and her father was a plantation owner. Marie grew up with the Catholic religion. She met Jacques Paris and married him in her local church in 1819. About a year later, Jacques mysteriously disappeared forever, leaving Marie to live on her own.

Tall and attractive, Marie began calling herself the Widow Paris. She became a hairdresser to support herself, traveling to important citizens' homes throughout New Orleans. As she listened to her clients, Marie learned many secrets. She also paid local servants to keep her informed on the happenings in the area—knowledge that could be used for her own purposes.

It was during this time that Marie began practicing voodoo. After learning some of the craft from the master, Dr. John, the Widow Paris added her own beliefs and practices. By age 35, Marie was New Orleans' most powerful voodoo queen.

For a fee, Laveau traveled to private homes to bring spells, potions, and gris-gris bags (charms) to those who could afford her price. Marie also told people's fortunes. Of course, telling people's future was much easier when she knew what was going on all around the city.

Below: The tomb of voodoo queen Marie Laveau in New Orleans, Louisiana.

Marie called on wives whose husbands were drawn to other women. The voodoo queen used her knowledge to "unhex" these husbands. There are no reports that she turned any wayward husbands into zombies, although Laveau did become famous for her public voodoo ceremonies, including dancing with Le Grand Zombi—a giant snake.

In the mid-1800s, Marie Laveau's daughter took up the voodoo queen's name and practice. The elderly Laveau finally passed away in June 1881, but the name "Marie Laveau" lived on with her child and is still revived by other voodooiennes even today.

Right: A modern-day voodoo queen.

DRUGS OF THE TRADE

Over the past 200 years, there have been hundreds of reports of zombies, people who appear to have no will of their own. This has resulted in modern-day researchers conducting professional studies of these strange occurrences.

Ethnobotanists are scientists who study plants and how they are used in medicine and religion in certain cultures. One trained ethnobotanist, Wade Davis, traveled to Haiti in 1982 to study how people could be turned into zombies. Davis collected and tested eight different zombie powders. The powders were all somewhat different, but four ingredients showed up repeatedly. Combined and given in the right dosage, these ingredients make a drug that turns people into zombies—still alive, but with no will of their own.

Puffer Fish

Puffer fish is known to contain a deadly toxin called tetrodotoxin. The eyes and internal organs of most puffer fish cause paralysis and death. It is estimated that a single puffer fish has enough poison

Above: A bandtail puffer.
Eating the eyes and internal organs of a puffer fish result in paralysis and death.

to kill 30 adults. However, in Japan and Korea, the rest of the meat is considered a delicacy. Applied in small doses, puffer fish toxin has also been used to relieve serious pain.

Marine Toad

This giant toad produces a highly toxic poison from glands behind its head. There have been a few reports of humans dying from the milky white poison. However, it is usually an unfortunate animal, such as a dog or cat, that bites the toad and dies.

Hyla Tree Frog

This tree-climbing frog oozes a non-deadly liquid. The substance is an irritant, but won't kill people. However, the irritation results in many tiny open sores. These openings in the skin may be enough to allow the zombie powder to enter a person's body.

Human Remains

Ground up bones, blood, and other parts of people are common ingredients in zombie powders.

Above: A marine toad, also called a cane toad, produces a milky white poison from glands behind its head.
Below: A Hyla tree frog.

A Recovered Zombie?

Clairvius Narcisse died on May 2, 1962, in a hospital in Port-au-Prince, Haiti. He had entered the hospital with a high fever and a great deal of pain. He also had trouble breathing. The very sick man finally slipped into a coma and died.

Two doctors declared Narcisse dead. His sister, Angelina, identified her brother's body. Another sister, Marie Claire, witnessed the death certificate, placing her fingerprint on the paper. The family buried the young man in a local cemetery. All that seemed to be left of Narcisse were memories.

Eighteen years later, in 1980, a man approached Angelina. He introduced himself as her brother. Angelina stared at the vacant-eyed man. She began to believe him. Friends and family members gathered, and they recognized him, too. How could this be possible?

Narcisse's story was strange, almost unbelievable. He claimed that he had been dug up from his grave and beaten awake by a master of black magic. Narcisse was led away to become a slave laborer on a remote sugar plantation. For years he stayed in a zombified state. Finally, his master died. Narcisse was able to regain his mind and escape.

According to Narcisse, the whole saga started when he had refused to sell land that his brothers wanted sold. They arranged for him to be zombified. A special poison was secretly given to Narcisse, which put him in a paralyzed, near-death state. The doctors at the hospital were completely fooled, and declared him dead. After Narcisse's burial, he was immediately dug up and revived by a zombie master. For years, the black magician kept Narcisse drugged, using him to work on the distant plantation. After the zombie slave owner died, Narcisse finally escaped the grueling farm work. The man did not return to his village until all the brothers who had caused Narcisse's horrific life had died.

Facing Page: A photo of Felicia Felix-Mentor. This Haiti resident reportedly died and was buried in 1907, but was found wandering the countryside in 1937, a story similar to what Clairvius Narcisse said happened to him.

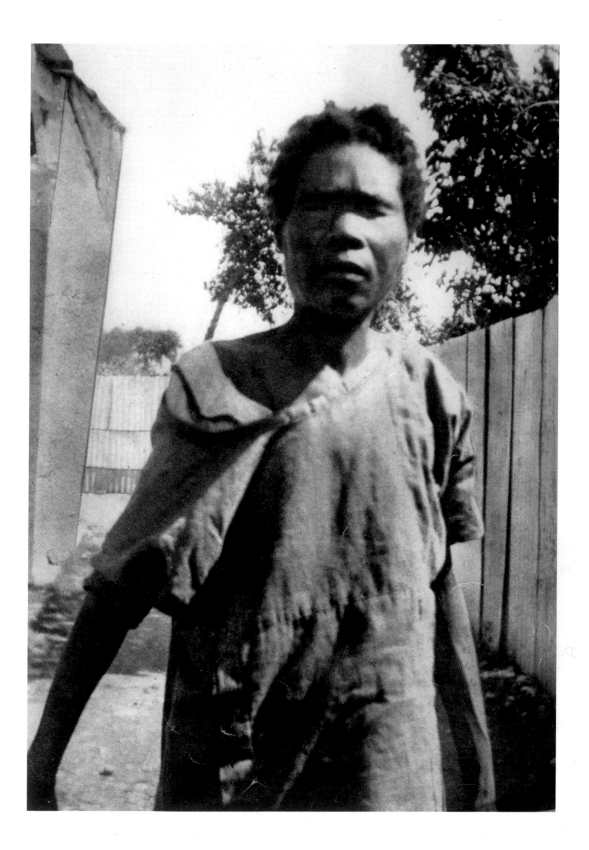

Many scientists dispute Narcisse's story, and other zombie stories like it. In some cases, it has been found that supposed zombies are, in fact, people with mental illnesses. Other "living dead" turn out to be cases of mistaken identity, people who happen to resemble those who have died.

However, scientists have confirmed the physical effects of tetrodotoxin on humans. This chemical, found in puffer fish, is a powerful poison. Puffer fish, also called blowfish, are found in many places worldwide, including the waters surrounding Haiti. Even small doses of tetrodotoxin can be fatal. Taken in the right amount, the poison leads to a rapid drop in body temperature. Muscles in the body stop responding. Breathing becomes difficult, then seems to stop altogether. Victims appear to be dead. Administering the precise amount of tetrodotoxin to people, without killing them, is tricky, to say the least. However, people who survive the poisoning do recover completely.

Today, there is a law in Haiti that makes it a crime to turn someone into a zombie. Article 249 states: *"It shall be qualified as attempted murder the employment which may be made against any person of substances which, without causing actual death, produce a lethargic coma more or less prolonged. If, after the administering of such substances, the person had been buried, the act shall be considered murder no matter what result follows."*

In other words, if someone drugs another person, buries them as though they were dead, then digs the person up and brings them back to life, it is still considered murder in Haiti.

Facing Page: A modern-day voodoo priest.
Below: A cemetery on the island of Haiti.

YAWS

Aside from black-magic drugs and powders, there is a medical condition that makes people look like zombies, and it often strikes at children. Yaws is a disease that usually infects young people in areas with hot temperatures, high humidity, and heavy rainfall. It is often found in places with poor sanitation and overcrowding, where infected people easily spread the disease through person-to-person contact.

The infection results in many sores, often on the face, legs, arms, and feet. The painful wounds on the bottoms of the feet sometimes cause a sufferer to walk in a slow, zombie-like shuffle.

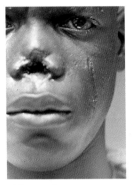

Above: A man stricken with yaws. The word "yaws" may have come from "yaya," the Caribbean word for sore.

Right: Crowded, unsanitary conditions and a warm, tropical climate can result in the spread of yaws, a disease that makes the sufferers look like zombies.

Yaws is easily curable with penicillin or other modern antibiotics, but if left untreated, the disease will spread across the body and worsen. The results are gruesome, with sickening bone, joint, and soft-tissue deformities. As they grow, young children stricken with the disease can be left with horrible disfigurements.

In the 1950s, as many as 25-150 million people suffered from yaws in Africa, Asia, South America, Central America, and the Pacific Islands. The disease was virtually unknown in North America, but stories and news reports eventually spread. It's easy to imagine how a sufferer's painful shuffle, open sores, and deformities could lead a Westerner to conclude that they were seeing a zombie. This, plus the ongoing fascination with voodoo, set the stage for creative minds to turn scientific fact into zombie fiction.

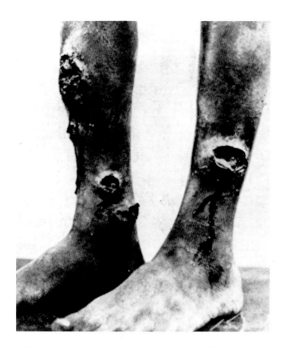

Above: Advanced yaws with painful, open sores. Sufferers also often have sores on the bottoms of their feet, which cause them to walk with a slow, zombie-like shuffle.

MOVIE ZOMBIES

Most people who watch horror movies love zombies. The decaying, plodding, unstoppable creatures are delightfully horrifying. From voodoo and black magic to radiation and toxic chemicals, the dead come to life on the movie screen as mean, gruesome, decomposing terrors.

White Zombie

This horror movie, made in 1932, is thought to be the first film to feature zombies. A young couple arrives in the tropical paradise of Haiti to be wed. However, a plantation owner is in love with the bride-to-be. He asks a local voodoo master (played by Bela Lugosi, the famous horror actor) to turn her into a zombie. He plans to revive her later, in order to keep her for himself.

Right: 1932's *White Zombie* is thought to be the first zombie movie. It starred Bela Lugosi, famous for his role as the vampire Dracula.

Night of the Living Dead

Released in 1968, this George A. Romero picture is universally credited as being the film from which all zombie movies today have their roots. Radiation from a fallen satellite brings dead people back to life—and they want to eat the living. A group of strangers hides in a farmhouse, desperately trying to keep the bloodthirsty zombies out. The movie was remade in 1990, plus a 3D version in 2006. Several sequels have also been made. In 1999, the United States Library of Congress added *Night of the Living Dead* to the National Film Registry, citing the film's historical and cultural importance.

Above: Director George A. Romero created the ultimate zombie movies. His first was the 1968 classic *Night of the Living Dead.* *Right:* Romero's original zombie movie and three of his sequels.

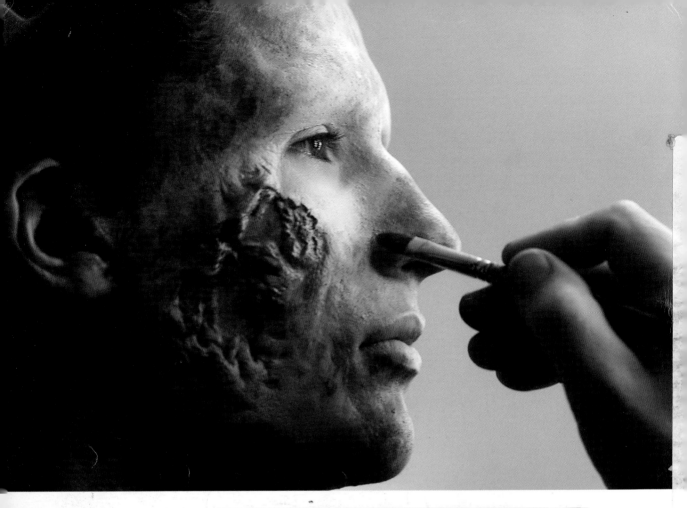

Above and Right: Actors receive final make-up touches for the filming of the 2005 film sequel to *Return of the Living Dead.* For some actors, application of the traditional zombie wounds, open sores, and hanging flesh can take hours.

Shaun of the Dead

Known as a "rom zom com," or romantic zombie comedy, this 2004 British film was a commercial success in both the United States and overseas. Written by Simon Pegg and Edgar Wright, the story centered on Shaun, an appliance salesman who tries to deal with problems surrounding his work, girlfriend, mother, stepfather, and best friend—all while handling his town's local zombie uprising. The film was written as a spoof honoring George A. Romero's *Night of the Living Dead.*

Above: A poster for the frightening, yet humorous, 2004 British zombie film *Shaun of the Dead.* The film stars writer Simon Pegg as the couch-potato-turned-zombie-hunter Shaun. The popular movie has been termed a "zomedy."

ZOMBIES IN GAMES

Zombies present excellent enemies in video and board games. Usually designed for teen or mature players, the gruesome and graphic games offer zombie opponents who leap out as hungry, flesh-eating living corpses.

Resident Evil

In this survival horror video game, the Raccoon City police team's Special Tactics and Rescue Squad (S.T.A.R.S) is called upon to investigate a series of murders. When the Bravo Team fails to come back, the Alpha Team is sent on a rescue mission. The Alpha Team discovers an abandoned mansion. Inside are their dead partners, as well as hordes of zombies and other evil creatures. Four versions of this popular game have been created, as well as several Hollywood movies, action figures, and a series of comic books.

Upper right: A *Resident Evil* game cover. *Below:* Characters from *Resident Evil*.

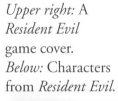

Stubbs the Zombie

In *Stubbs the Zombie in Rebel Without a Pulse*, video gamers take on a reverse role, playing Edward "Stubbs" Stubblefield, a former traveling salesman who has been turned into a zombie. The city of Punchbowl has been built over Stubbs' grave, and he's not happy about it. The undead salesman eats human brains to gain life and flings his own detachable head at humans, sometimes turning them into zombies in the process. Punchbowl is a city in a full-scale human vs. zombie war.

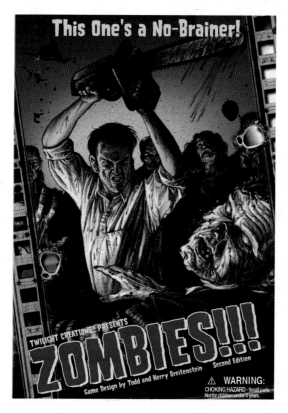

Above: Screen shots of *Stubbs the Zombie.*

Zombies!!!®

Any board game that comes with 100 plastic zombies has to be fun—right?! The objective of *Zombies!!!* (left) is to either make it to the center of the board by escaping the zombie hordes or to collect 25 zombies. This is an imaginative role-playing game based on classic zombie movies.

ZOMBIES IN BOOKS

People's fascination with zombies has found a place in fiction, nonfiction, and comic books. Since the 19th century, the odd, gruesome, and often terrifying world of zombies and their masters has filled thousands of pages while keeping readers entertained and frightened.

The Magic Island

In the late 1920s, American author William B. Seabrook traveled to the island of Haiti. His experiences with black magic and the voodoo religion were vividly detailed in the popular book *The Magic Island*. This is believed to have been the first book to introduce zombies to Western culture. Seabrook's detailed accounts inspired the 1932 film *White Zombie*.

The Zombie Survival Guide: Complete Protection From the Living Dead

Written by Max Brooks and published in 2003, this fictional instruction manual gives all the necessary details for surviving a zombie uprising. Brooks provides instructions for recognizing a zombie, knowing its strengths and weaknesses, and how the living should protect themselves from the living dead. *The Zombie Survival Guide* is a serious look at a frightening fictional topic.

Marvel Zombies

What if all the Marvel superheroes were infected with a virus from outer space, and each powerful hero became one of the super undead? This is exactly what happened in *Marvel Zombies*. This unique comic book mini-series came out in December 2005 with infectious popularity. The phrase "Marvel Zombies" was a negative term used to identify Marvel Comics fans. This series put the name up front—and the human-hungry power zombies were after anyone not yet infected. The covers of each of the five issues were cleverly zombified versions of other famous Marvel issues.

Above: Beginning in 2005, Marvel Comics created a series of comic books entitled *Marvel Zombies*, in which classic superheroes were turned into zombies.

GLOSSARY

3D MOVIE
A movie filmed with a certain technique so that it presents an illusion of depth, or three dimensions, to the viewer.

CARIBBEAN
The islands and area of the Caribbean Sea, roughly the area between Florida and South and Central America.

COMA
A state of prolonged and deep unconsciousness caused by disease, injury, or poison. Those in a coma do not respond to attempts to "wake" them.

ETHNOBOTANIST
A scientist who studies the relationship between plants and people. An ethnobotanist learns how different civilizations have used plants for food, medicine, cosmetics and other purposes, as well as in religious and cultural practices.

GRIS-GRIS
An amulet or charm used to ward off evil, or bring good fortune.

LIBRARY OF CONGRESS
Established in 1800, the United States Library of Congress serves as the research arm of the U.S. Congress and is the largest library in the world, with more than 130 million items. The Library's mission is "to make its resources available and useful to the Congress and the American people and to sustain and preserve a universal collection of knowledge and creativity for future generations."

LOA
The spirits of the voodoo (or vodou) religion practiced in Haiti and other parts of the world. Loas are not gods, but intermediaries between the creator and humanity. Loas are to be served, and each has their own personal likes and dislikes, as well as individual sacred rhythms, songs, and dances.

MULATTO
The offspring of one black parent and one white parent. Also, more generally, a person of mixed white and black ancestry.

PLANTATION

A large farm or agricultural estate located in a warm climate, such as the Caribbean or the southern United States. In the 18th and 19th centuries, the workers on plantations were primarily slaves who were housed on the estate.

VOODOO/VODOU

A religion begun in Haiti by slaves brought from Africa. It combines elements of many religions, and uses rites from several ethnic groups. One type of voodoo includes the practice of zombification.

Below: Michael Jackson stands with dancers dressed as zombies from the popular 1983 music video *Thriller*. Award-winning special effects artist Richard Baker created the make-up.

INDEX

Below: Shaun of the Dead *poster. A "zomedy."*